Delegati

About the series

Fast Track is a series of short, practical guides designed to get you up to speed on key business and management skills.

Written by experts with many years' experience in the field, each guide gives you instant access to key tips, advice and guidance – information you can put to work straightaway.

First six titles in the series
  Appraisal & Performance Management 1 85835 948 1
  Delegation 1 85835 953 8
  Leadership 1 85835 963 5
  Managing Attendance 1 85835 968 6
  Managing Conflict 1 85835 978 3
  Managing Time 1 85835 958 9

About the Series Editor
Andrew Forrest is Director of Learning and Development at The Industrial Society. He has over 30 years' experience working with and developing people.

Delegation

Andrew Forrest

First published in 2001
Reprinted 2002
The Industrial Society
Robert Hyde House
48 Bryanston Square
London W1H 2EA
Telephone: +44 (0)870 400 1000

© The Industrial Society 2001

ISBN 1 85835 953 8

British Library Cataloguing-in-Publication Data.
A catalogue record for this book is available from the
British Library.

Printed by: Cromwell Press
Cover image by: Digital Vision
Cover design by: Sign Design
The Industrial Society is a Registered Charity No. 290003

Contents

Introduction

Whether your job title is manager, team leader or supervisor – if you have people reporting to you, you are in a position to delegate.

Delegation is a powerful tool; not only can it free up your time to work on the tasks that really matter, but it can also provide a great opportunity for your delegate to gain in knowledge, experience and confidence – if used correctly!

Packed with practical advice, guidance and real-life insights, this book outlines the essentials of successful delegation, helping you – and your delegate – to gain maximum benefit.

What is delegation?

This chapter covers:
> What is delegation? – a definition.
> Matching authority.
> Beyond delegation to empowerment.

"They want me to make decisions but there are so many areas where I don't have the authority".

"Senior management won't let supervisors make decisions; everything has to be rubber-stamped by them. The supervisors end up lacking in confidence and this shows in their attitude to work".

These comments, from two different organisations, are typical of many. Senior managers complain of being overworked, while employees lower down want to show what they can do, but are stifled. In these organisations delegation just isn't happening.

Before investigating why, we first need to distinguish exactly what delegation means.

Delegation

Delegation is not simply a matter of allocating duties, none of which you would be expected to carry out yourself. Delegation involves conscious choice. If you are in a position to delegate, delegation occurs when you choose to entrust a colleague with a specific task which you could have retained yourself. This task could be a 'one-off' or one which will become a regular feature of that person's work.

Whatever your job title, if you have people reporting to you, you are in a position to delegate. It may be, however, that you are reluctant to do so. This could be for a number of reasons. Perhaps you have had unfortunate experiences with it in the past, or you are worried it will take too much time; you may even have a niggling concern that your less experienced colleague might find a better method of doing the work than you have used yourself! All of these are common and understandable concerns. We will investigate them further in the next chapter.

It is hard to find an elegant word to describe the person on the receiving end of delegation. 'Subordinate' is certainly not the right word; it belongs to an earlier era and implies inferiority. The most appropriate term seems to be the 'delegate', so that is what we will use.

Adequate authority

If you have decided to delegate something, you cannot just hand it over like a parcel. The key ingredient which must accompany the task is *adequate authority* to achieve it. As an example, suppose you need to fill a vacancy in your team and you ask a colleague to handle it. You may decide on partial delegation, ie the delegate's task is to go through all the candidates' application forms, select a shortlist for interview and leave you to make the final choice between the two best candidates. In this case, the authority required by the delegate will be to sift the applications on their own; to conduct shortlist interviews with a colleague; to select the final two candidates; and to write letters to all unsuccessful candidates.

On the other hand, you may decide to delegate the whole task. If so, the authority given to your delegate needs to go beyond the steps listed above to encompass the final selection of the best candidate, including negotiating the salary and employment package, taking up references, issuing a contract of employment and devising an induction programme. It is really frustrating to your delegate if, having delegated the task to them, you then keep breathing down their neck and half-reclaiming the necessary authority.

Empowerment

The stage beyond delegation is that of *empowerment*. The crucial difference is that if you *delegate* something your delegate has to achieve it, even though their method of doing so may differ from yours. If you *empower* them, however, they have the additional authority to decide whether the task should be carried out at all: they may choose to discontinue it. For example, if you feel that the way that the annual stocktaking is carried out is unwieldy, you may delegate to one of your team the task of reviewing and improving it. But if you *empower* them, you have given them the additional possibility of deciding that you do not need annual stocktaking at all – the time and trouble involved are not worthwhile, so you will abandon the whole system and control stock in some other way.

Whether the task in question is large or small, you should clarify the limits of your delegate's authority. A very useful guideline is to be explicit about *destination* rather than route: the delegate must be clear about what end result you require, then they can find their own way towards it.

So we have now defined the two key words:

Delegation means entrusting a colleague with a task which you could have retained yourself. The colleague (the 'delegate') must be given adequate authority to carry out the task.

Empowerment means transferring accountability, authority and resources to those people who are closest to the task, within a supportive 'blame-free' culture.

Summary checklist

✓ Clarify the real meaning of delegation.

✓ Avoid using the term 'subordinate'.

✓ Give adequate authority.

✓ Consider empowerment.

Difficulties in, and barriers to, delegation

This chapter considers:
> What stops delegation in its tracks.
> Six common barriers to delegation and how to tackle them.

As we will see, the actual process of delegating is not particularly complicated. The greatest difficulty which people encounter about delegation is their reluctance to embark on it in the first place! This reluctance can take several forms; below we consider six of the most common barriers to delegation.

Six common barriers to delegation

1 " I can't risk it because you will get it wrong"

This can be a self-defeating argument, because you can't know that a person will get it wrong if they've never been given the chance to get it right.

The answer takes us back to chapter 1: matching accountability with authority, and forward to chapter 4: clarifying boundaries.

Obviously, you will not delegate a task to anyone if you genuinely consider that the risk of failure vastly outweighs the chance of success.

But in most cases, give them the benefit of the doubt and remember how you came up trumps earlier in your own career when your manager had faith in you.

2 "I could show you how to do it, but in the short term it will take more time than if I do it myself"

I am afraid this excuse is well beyond its sell-by date! In using it, you are assuming that if you hold on a little longer a quiet spell will magically appear in your workload, giving you time to coach someone. The pace of change is such that there are no quiet spells around the corner any more. So: coach the person now – but bear in mind that the coaching need not involve one big chunk of time; it may well be possible to spread it over two or three short sessions, which do not make such great in-roads into your diary.

3 "I don't want to hand over this activity – I've always done it myself"

This is another way of saying that the activity is within your comfort zone and it would make you vulnerable to let go of it.

This is a really dangerous line to take because it is fossilising your job – on this basis your work will be just the same five years from now; or more likely, your job will not exist then because it will have been overtaken by events. So, in your own interests, abandon this reasoning quickly!

4 "I don't want to hand over this activity because you may overtake me"

The roots of this attitude lie in the past, at a time when promotion was almost always vertical within a given function – so senior managers might notice an individual at a lower level beginning to outstrip their own manager.

This argument is now doubly invalid. Traditional career 'silos' are much less common, and the manager who fails to delegate is effectively condemning themselves to operating below their 'added value' level. Nowadays you are much more likely to be recognised for your skill in developing your people, so if promotion is your aim delegate as much as you can. Several effective leaders have said that one of their principles is to recruit people who are cleverer than themselves.

5 "I can't delegate this because policy doesn't allow it to be carried out below my level"

There are some good reasons why authority to take specific actions is retained at a given level. These can include confidentiality, legal requirements (eg only directors can do X or Y), prevention of fraud (eg cheque signatories) and so on.

But in other cases the grounds for keeping authority at a particular level may be no more valid than "It's always been that way". At some time in the past someone relatively junior made a wrong judgement, and in a typical piece of over-reaction senior managers decreed that the decision must be taken higher up – and there it has remained. It is likely to stick there, permanently inhibiting initiative, until you challenge it. A large financial services company used to have a level of management so set in their ways about retaining authority that they were known as 'the permafrost'. So don't get icebound – thaw out.

6 "I don't want to hand over this activity – I enjoy it too much"

Now at least you are being honest! Handing over some activities can be a genuine wrench, particularly if you have created them yourself from scratch. Owner-managers of small businesses often come to grief over this.

In this situation, you have the right to expect some sensitivity on the part of your delegate. If you are going to hand over something very dear to your heart, such as leading an activity which was your own brainchild, your delegate should be careful not to grab it greedily. You cannot expect them to handle the activity in the same way as yourself: indeed, there may come a time when they decide to discontinue it.

The principle which you should both use is: fit for purpose. By handing over this activity you have released some time in which to deliver your own added value to the organisation – you have created a better match between your talents and the organisation's needs. And at the same time, your delegate approaches the activity with fresh eyes, and enhances the possibility of the activity becoming a better fit with the organisation's current priorities.

Summary checklist

✓ Face your fears about delegating.

✓ Delegation is in your own best interest too.

Opportunities for delegation

This chapter covers:
> The three 'zones of experience'.
> Using vacancies as an opportunity.
> Using maternity leave as an opportunity.
> Your 'added value' level.
> '5-way management'.
> Your efficiency damaged by 'clutter and hassle'.

Delegation not only frees up your time, but it also offers your delegate the opportunity to expand their skills and knowledge. The following diagram illustrates how a delegate might experience new tasks – the three 'zones of experience'.

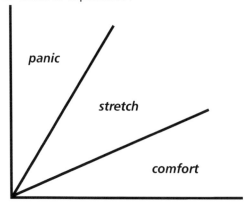

The three zones of experience

1 The 'comfort' zone

In the delegate's 'comfort' zone will be those aspects of their work in which they are reasonably experienced and confident.

2 The 'stretch' zone

In the 'stretch' zone they are testing their ability on unfamiliar tasks, or trying to improve in some aspect of the job which they may not much enjoy but which they cannot escape.

3 The 'panic' zone

The 'panic' zone will be rarely visited, they hope: it houses work whose sheer volume is unmanageable, or which takes them well beyond their skills.

The zone where they will learn most is, of course, the 'stretch' zone. If they stay in that zone for too long they are likely to edge towards panic, so they should move back into their comfort zone at intervals to gather their strength and wits, ready for their next excursion into the 'stretch' area.

An obvious opportunity for you to help your delegate explore these zones is when you are away on holiday, or on a training course or business trip. During these absences the delegate can deputise for you. They will learn nothing if you merely expect them to act as a cipher or notetaker – you should delegate as much authority as you judge they can handle. A good guideline is for you to enter your own 'stretch' zone when deciding your delegate's authority level.

So, for example, during your absence they will attend a regular meeting in your place. They should be able to make decisions in this meeting in your name; not provisional decisions which you have to confirm on your return, but full decisions, otherwise you are slowing up the whole decision-making process for the organisation. In the same way, they should be able to spend money within your budget, and challenge an individual's performance if required.

To enable the delegate to do these things, you should make known to those concerned – everyone in your team, and others beyond – the extent of the delegate's authority, to avoid misunderstandings or embarrassment. On your return you should expect them to give you a full debriefing, not only of what has happened but also what they have learned from it, and any aspects where the delegate may now feel ready to make the transfer of accountability permanent.

Vacancies

Whenever a vacancy occurs in your team, for whatever reason (a person being promoted, or transferred to another department, or retiring, etc), there is the opportunity to rethink that role from scratch.

Suppose you didn't fill the post at all – what would suffer? Could you revise the role to a more junior level, and transfer part of it to someone else? Or could you upgrade the role and provide more scope for someone? Or should you carry out a reshuffle between the vacant post and three or four neighbouring posts, shaping them around people's skills?

It is very easy for posts to become fixed in our minds, so that when Brenda or Philip leaves we recruit their clones. Instead, each vacancy as it occurs provides scope for constant refreshment of your team, including progressive delegation from yourself.

Maternity leave

Maternity leave may offer another chance for delegation. Maternity leave has the advantage of spanning a predictable length of time – several months during which the expectant mother's work can be delegated to a colleague. This version of delegation is different, however. When the mother returns to work and resumes her old job, the colleague may feel disappointed if she or he has to revert back to 'lower level' work.

So you should discuss this with the people concerned, preferably *before* maternity leave begins.

Options

The options for the mother's return could include:

- The two people resume their previous roles with no change. The 'deputy' has a debriefing discussion with you to establish what he or she has learned from the experience.

- You make some adjustments to the jobs of both people, to make a better fit with their skills. For example, it is quite common for a mother to wish to move from full-time to part-time work once she has new parental responsibilities.

- If the deputy has gained new knowledge, skills and confidence from the experience, he or she may be ready to make a permanent move into a new role, eg by applying for an internal promotion.

The other step which can be taken to make the most of the maternity leave opportunity is for the expectant mother to brief and coach her colleague in good time before starting her leave.

'Added value'

The most important reason for delegating is to enable you to operate at your optimum level of effectiveness. Carla Brown puts this very well: "When a £25-an-hour manager does a £10-an-hour job, the company is short-changed £15."(See Further Reading).

The tough test, which we should all regularly impose on ourselves, is to ask: "Am I operating at my true level?" If you are honest with yourself when you look back on a week's work, you may well find that for an uncomfortable proportion of the time you have worked below that level – doing things which did not require your experience, double-checking work already done, and so on.

The best way to focus on your 'added value' is to split it into two parts: your role and yourself.

First, your role: what are the key outcomes which the role is designed to achieve? If your role did not exist, what would suffer? What difference is your role supposed to make?

Secondly, yourself: the chances of your being a 'perfect fit' with your role are slight. There may be elements within your role at which you are not particularly skilled – can these be transferred to someone else at your level, or are they opportunities for delegation? I am not suggesting that you offload all of the parts of your role which you don't particularly enjoy! But it is surely intelligent rather than irresponsible to consider which of these elements to retain and which to transfer.

If you are making your full contribution to the organisation, it is as though you were placing two parcels on the table.

The first parcel contains everything which enables you to carry out your role – including your professional training, your experience, your authority over resources such as money and equipment, and so on.

The second parcel contains skills, abilities, enthusiasms and talents which you happen to possess as a person but which are not automatic

Two parcels

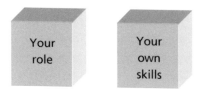

to your role. For example, you can speak Italian but the role does not demand this; you are very experienced in project planning but projects do not feature in your current job; you have considerable knowledge of local government derived from a post earlier in your career, but this knowledge isn't directly needed in your current role, etc.

You are thus able to offer your colleagues the contents of not one but *two* parcels. Intelligent senior managers realise the potential of this approach, and make sure that people are not too modest about parcel number two.

They also encourage people to regard the contents of both parcels as resources available beyond department boundaries – at the disposal of the whole organisation.

You owe it to your colleagues to make sure that they are aware of your personal skills; they owe it to you to make sensible adjustments to the boundaries of your role so that you can bring these skills to bear.

You are delivering your true added value when you are operating at the full potential both of your role and of your personal skills. The process of establishing this added value will yield delegation opportunities.

Exercise

Imagine you are the business development manager of an office supplies company. You have six direct reports: four development executives, a researcher and a team administrator. At present about 20% of your time is spent monitoring your team's results, which involves statistical analysis of sales leads, customer feedback and so on. You are confident in this aspect of your work and enjoy subjecting the figures to scrutiny.

You have recently undergone 360% feedback as an extension of the company's traditional appraisal scheme. This included

> *comments from each member of your team and from some key customers. This has revealed that your customers particularly value your face-to-face contact with them, while your development executives strongly appreciate being coached by you, such as during joint visits to customers. What does this feedback teach you? Are you using your time effectively? Are you 'adding value'?*

This feedback should make you realise that your true added value lies in direct customer contact and in coaching, rather than in close monitoring of results. So, perhaps you should switch 10% of your time to these two activities, and delegate the statistical analysis to your researcher and administrator: they can present you with the outcomes of the analysis, instead of you carrying out the analysis personally.

'5-way management'

Another route towards delegation is '5-way management'.
   Look at each of these dimensions in turn, starting with 'Managing upwards'.

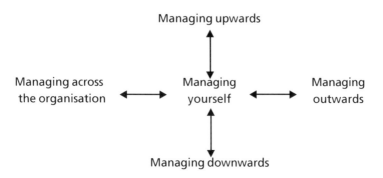

Managing upwards

Managing across the organisation

Managing yourself

Managing outwards

Managing downwards

Managing upwards

Is your own manager retaining some activity which you feel able to take over? Are there decisions which you feel able to make, which you always have to take to your manager for approval? Does waiting for a green light from above create a series of red lights for you – and for the members of your team? Are there issues which in theory have been delegated to you, but which in practice your manager meddles in and checks?

Getting delegation to work well is not limited to yourself and those below you – you may well need a dialogue with your own manager as well.

Managing outwards

'Managing outwards' may also be a fruitful source of delegation opportunities. Are you personally dealing with some customers or suppliers whom one of your team could now take over? When regulators, auditors or inspectors send you their reports, do you have to read them line by line or could you ask one of your team to take this on, summarising the key points for your attention?

Managing downwards

'Managing downwards' is the most obvious area for delegation opportunities. Just as you have cross-examined yourself on the 'added value' concept, ask each of your team to do the same and to make 'bids' to take over some of your work. You will have to judge whether these bids are realistic, but delegating the search for delegation opportunities is surely irresistible!

Managing across the organisation

'Managing across the organisation' involves all your relationships with other departments. Are there departments whose understanding of your team's work is inadequate and which results in frustration and delays? Should you be spending more of your time improving these relationships – and if so, could you create this time by delegating some other aspect of your work?

The 5-way management model helps you to redistribute your time in the most effective way.

Managing yourself

The final area of 5-way management is 'Managing yourself'. You have already covered this to some extent through the added value test. Your workload should therefore consist mainly of issues which really do require your personal attention – in other words, you are being *effective*. The remaining question then is "Are you being *efficient*?"

Two things can impede your efficiency: hassle and clutter. Hassle means other people making you inefficient; clutter means self-inflicted inefficiency of any kind – not just an untidy desk. Here are a few examples and advice on what you can do about them.

- **Hassle – other people making you inefficient:** you owe it to yourself to have some peace and quiet to think and plan. To avoid this being sabotaged by constant interruptions, create a time during the working day when you will accept no telephone calls or meetings, however brief. Half an hour a day can work wonders. Your team members and colleagues will gradually realise that you really mean it – but make sure you return their calls promptly at the end of your 'sacred time'.

- **Requests for data:** other departments in your organisation may bombard you with demands for data. If this becomes burdensome, explore why they need it. It may be possible to negotiate less frequent submissions or 'approximate but rapid' as an alternative to 'spot-on accurate but slower', or to manage by exception, ie only to have to supply data if whatever you are monitoring has gone outside normal limits.

- **Status:** your attempts to delegate may not be appreciated by colleagues at your level in other departments. They may feel slighted if you no longer attend meetings but one of your team goes in your place. It may be best to pre-empt this by explaining to them at the outset why you are taking this action: namely, because you can deliver greater added value to the organisation by a different activity, and that you have given adequate authority to your delegate to contribute fully to the meetings. This might even persuade your colleagues to do likewise – so you are pushing the decision-making further down the organisation.

- **Clutter – self-imposed inefficiency:** much of this revolves around time management and your best step is to read my colleague Debra Allcock Tyler's book in this series (see Further Reading). It covers issues such as 'bring forward' files, diary planning, how to deal with papers, etc. Time management is partly about techniques, but much more about attitude – your own determination to control your work, and not let it control you.

Summary checklist

✓ Use the stretch zone.

✓ Use vacancies to reshape roles.

✓ Try out deputies during maternity leave.

✓ Exploit both your role and your own talents.

✓ Use all of the dimensions in 5-way management.

✓ Tackle hassle and clutter.

Establishing boundaries

> This chapter explores:
> > The boundaries within which delegates can operate.

Boundaries

Delegation is not a licence to be irresponsible, nor should it be constrained by a lack of the necessary authority. When you decide to delegate something to a member of your team, it is helpful to use a simple checklist of the resources which may be necessary for the delegation to be successful. These will form the boundaries within which your delegate can operate. They may include:

Finance

If the delegated work already has a budget, all you need to do is pass the authority for that budget over to the delegate. If the delegated work is a one-off, the delegate needs to be clear at the outset where the money will come from and what spending limits they must observe.

Buildings, office space, etc

If the delegated task is that of reorganising three teams into a different configuration, are there implications about space, furnishings, etc? For example, if the delegate has never before changed the layout of an office, it is easy to overlook costs such as additional computer cabling.

Consumable materials

Sometimes a delegated task can involve trying out a new way of working as a pilot. If so, you may need to write off some material which will be consumed at the trial stage.

Time

A deadline date for completion of the task will normally be set automatically. If the task is major, or will take several weeks or months to complete, it may also be useful to agree milestones towards it – eg, a first progress report after x weeks, a second after y weeks, and so on. But if you and your delegate decide on these milestones, please do not add a whole series of extra milestones by constant checking! *Milestones* should not become *millstones* around someone's neck.

People

Your delegate will be able to carry out some delegated tasks on their own. But some tasks may require them to have authority to use various colleagues – perhaps including some beyond your immediate team, such as members of a project team.

Whatever resources are involved, the guideline is the same: clarify the boundaries of the delegate's authority over them, then leave them to tackle the task in their own way.

Case study

Sometimes when a team becomes stuck on a problem, it helps if they remind themselves of the boundaries.

I was facilitating a workshop for a project team who had to plan a complex move of the organisation's head office to another site, with knock-on effects including the introduction of teleworking and some potential redundancies. They were stuck; no matter which starting point they chose, they soon ran into blockages.

So we took a step back and listed all the boundaries for the project – we called them the 'givens'. These were the facts which could not be changed, no matter what. The list included:

- The overall budget for the project.

- The date for the announcement to employees on which departments would move to each floor of the new building.

- The deadline by which everyone must have moved out of the present building, etc.

For the project team members, this reminder of the boundaries produced the space within which they could create options, and the workshop made headway from that point onwards.

Summary checklist

✓ Use a list of resources as a guide to the boundaries of delegation.

5

Creating the right climate for delegation

> This chapter covers:
> > Building trust and creating the right climate.
> > Different types of mistakes.
> > Factors within your delegate's control, and those outside.
> > Creating the right climate for delegation.

Delegation involves letting go, so it is bound to be somewhat scary for both you – the manager – and the delegate. One dictionary defines "to delegate" as "to entrust a task to another person in whom one has confidence". Trust and confidence cannot co-exist with extensive checking, still less with a blame culture.

Creating the right climate

So what steps can you take to create the right climate?

- Remember some of the mistakes you have made yourself, particularly when you were learning the ropes in your first job in charge of a team. If you were lucky enough to have a manager who didn't come down heavily on you for mistakes, but helped you to learn from them, that is exactly what you can do for your delegate now.

- Discuss with your team the difference between negligent or reckless mistakes – such as those endangering health and safety, or the organisation's intellectual property, or large amounts of money – and 'sensible' mistakes where a person uses their initiative but gets it wrong. The penalty for the first group will be severe, and rightly so; your response to the second may well be to hold a constructive '*post-mortem*' with the whole team, so that everyone can learn from the experience.

- Coach your delegate in understanding the factors which are within their control and those which are not. At the organisational level, a company can not influence changes in interest rates or the strength of the pound, or what new products a competitor may launch.

Issues for the delegate

What are the relevant issues at your delegate's level? They are likely to include the following:

- The delegate cannot change company policy (at least not single-handed and overnight).

- Although the task which you have delegated is extremely important to your delegate, it is extremely unlikely to be the top priority of every other department. The delegate cannot expect everyone to revise their priorities to suit them; but you can help the delegate to set their task within the context of the other departments' agendas so that its completion brings good results to all.

- When something goes wrong, it is very easy for managers to become very exercised about it and to formulate rules and procedures to prevent it ever happening again. For major mistakes this may be justified. For minor ones, however, it will almost certainly prove to be overkill. Besides organisation-wide policies, each department develops its own tangled thickets of procedures and regulations, like a golf course where 'out of bounds' is forever encroaching on the fairway. How much better to cut down the thickets and treat people as civilised and trustworthy. Of course, this will not prevent people from sometimes doing the most remarkably stupid things, but it sets people free to use their creativity on achieving delegated tasks, not on circumventing fussy rules and regulations.

A really basic point which you should make explicit with members of your team is that asking for help is not a sign of weakness, but simply common sense. A few years ago a financial services company had a slogan: 'Training is for wimps.' This kind of macho nonsense doesn't fool anyone. We all get out of our depth from time to time, or have a log jam of tasks, or need a second opinion. As the manager of the team, you can lead by example and ask your team for help when you need it.

To create the right climate for delegation you have to ensure that the members of your team feel confident – confident in themselves, in each other and in you as their manager. Your role is to provide this confidence through the various methods described in this book.

The confidence will be evident in three ways: they will feel **allowed** to make decisions, feel **motivated** to make decisions and have the relevant **skills** to make these decisions.

What, why and how

In his excellent book *Managing the Professional Service Firm* (see Further Reading), David Maister says:

> "*In managing the work of others, in any environment, one can choose to focus either on:*

WHAT is to be done;

HOW it is to be done;

or

WHY it is to be done.

In the management of professionals the leader should be very clear on the what (provide clear goals);

spend only the bare minimum of time on the how (involve them in the decision making, provide autonomy);

and spend a lot of time on the why (provide meaning)."

These three simple words, **what, why** and **how**, provide ideal guidance for the process of delegation. You have decided to delegate a task to a colleague. In briefing them about it, you will make the 'what' clear – the nature of the task, the outcomes required, the boundaries.

You are likely to tell them too little 'why' and too much 'how'. They will benefit from 'why' in the sense of why you feel that they are now ready to take on this task for the first time – this will boost their confidence. But they should also understand the 'why' in the sense of what David Maister calls "provide meaning". Why is this task significant? Why does it matter? It is this understanding which will convert your colleague's attitude from acquiescence to commitment.

Your delegate's understanding of the 'why' will also make it much easier for them to enlist the co-operation of other departments in carrying the task through to a successful conclusion.

So, dwell on the 'why', but go easy on the 'how'. So long as your delegate achieves the task within the agreed boundaries, you should not use your valuable time elaborating how they should approach it.

The humblest task can become energising if the person involved sees that it will make a difference. If you are arranging a high-powered conference, it really makes a difference if someone checks that the conference papers do not contain blemishes or misprints. It really makes a difference if someone tidies up the conference hall during every break in the programme. Such tasks are not glamorous, but they are important to the success of the event, and the people who carry them out should not be taken for granted but acknowledged.

Summary checklist

✓ Give guidance to your team on mistakes and on asking for help.

✓ Put more emphasis on 'why' than 'how'; give your delegate space.

6

Accountable and responsible

This chapter covers:
> Your delegate's role and their broader responsibility.
> A new look at job descriptions.

Roles and responsibilities

You have employed each member of your team to carry out a specific role. But as employees of the organisation they have a wider allegiance than just their role, because they have access to the organisation's resources: finance, buildings and equipment, consumable materials, time, reputation and goodwill, knowledge and people. They are both *accountable* and *responsible*.

Accountability means acceptance of a personal commitment to deliver results in a defined area of work.

Responsibility means acceptance of a duty to make effective use of all resources, and to enhance them where possible. Every employee in an organisation can be either responsible or irresponsible in their use of resources.

Job descriptions

An essential tool for a person's accountability is their job description. This may be written in the form of key result areas, or objectives and standards, or some similar terminology. Job descriptions often miss the opportunity to be dynamic and energising, and instead read as a dreary list of duties.

The key to converting them into much more exciting documents is to enhance the 'why' and if possible cut down on the 'how'. The job description should read **as a challenge to the job holder to make a difference**. It should convey the destination they are to reach, and leave them some scope to select the route.

In drafting a job description, you may find it useful to do so 'from the outside in', ie not a rehash of the way this job has always looked, but a revision based on the needs of the stakeholders for the job, both internal and external. If this job did not exist, would any stakeholders suffer? The external stakeholders could be suppliers, customers, clients, patients, regulators, the community. The internal stakeholders could be adjoining departments, or branches, or other business units, etc. It is instructive to consider the job through their eyes because the justification for this post is that it makes a difference to them.

Examples of behaving 'responsibly'

- You are walking through an office (not your own) and a telephone rings. There is no one in the office. Rather than ignore the phone, you answer it and try to help the caller.

- You are lucky enough to have an office of your own, but quite often your work takes you away for half a day or a full day at a time. Rather than have your office unused, you make it available to colleagues for meetings or as a place to work quietly without interruptions.

- You are off duty, out with friends. Someone makes a disparaging comment about your organisation, based on ill-informed gossip. You don't ignore it, or laugh it off, because your organisation's reputation is being damaged: you correct the misinformation.

- Your team has found a way of saving time in carrying out a process. You don't keep this to yourself, but take the initiative to share the knowledge with other teams so that they can replicate the savings.

Summary checklist

✓ Be a role model for accountability and responsibility.

✓ Ensure that job descriptions are dynamic.

7

How to delegate

This chapter covers:
> Learning styles.
> Gradual delegation, treating each individual appropriately.
> Delegating to a secretary/PA.
> Seven degrees of consultation.

Learning styles

In recent years, we have slowly but surely realised that people learn in different ways, and that this can have a considerable influence on how readily people respond to delegation opportunities. Peter Honey and Alan Mumford (see Further Reading) showed that there are four styles of learning.

The four styles of learning

1. An **activist** relishes being thrown in at the deep end and doesn't mind making mistakes.

2. A **pragmatist's** main concern is the practical application of what he or she has learned.

3. A **theorist** needs to put learning in context.

4. A **reflector** wants time in which to absorb learning, and doesn't like being rushed – the reverse of an activist.

Each of us has a preference for one or two of these four styles. It is not a question of one style being more efficient than the others – they are all valid.

If you are an activist and delegate something to a team member on a 'sink or swim' basis they may well panic. So you need to be aware of your own learning style as well as theirs. But this doesn't mean that they are 'stuck' with their natural preference. If a person only learns in one way they are cramping their effectiveness. All of us should be trying to expand our learning into the areas which are not our first choices. So a theorist should be encouraged to have a go, and not be over-cautious; just as an activist should sometimes learn by reading an article or a book, rather than always using the trial and error approach.

Gradual delegation

If you are planning to delegate a task which occurs fairly often, you may be able to hand it over gradually. Thus, on the first occasion, you carry out the task and the delegate observes, followed by a debriefing to enrich their understanding. The second time, they carry out the task with you observing – again followed by a debriefing. At this stage, remember the difference between destination and route: they may perform the task in a different way to you, but so long as they achieve the right outcome, does that matter?

After this second occasion, you may feel that they are ready to take over the task without needing you to observe them. It may be enough that when they first carry out the task alone they simply let you know afterwards: 'mission accomplished'.

A very useful method of gradual delegation was pioneered by BICC, the electronics and construction company. It works best where your delegate is in charge of a team of people, rather than being a sole operator such as a sales representative or a project engineer.

Here is how it works:

You ask one of your direct reports to write down all the decisions which *regularly* crop up in their job (this does not include 'one off' special situations). It is convenient if these are clustered under themes, eg the 'Staffing' list might include items such as 'Recruit staff up to grade 4 within budgeted numbers'; 'Authorise overtime working,' etc.

Alongside the list they should draw three columns headed 'Recommend', 'Act' and 'Delegate'.

The two of you then go through the whole list and agree for each item a tick to go in one of the three columns, which are self-explanatory: 'Recommend' means that when this decision arises your direct report comes to you with a recommended course of action but may not go further without your agreement; 'Act' simply means that they make the decision themselves; 'Delegate' means that they are transferring the decision to someone below their level, so the decision need no longer appear on their own list.

The R/A/D system

JOB TASK	RECOMMEND	ACT	DELEGATE
Budgeting figures	✓		
Training schedule			✓
Stationery supplies		✓	

For all these decisions the intention is steadily to push them towards the right: R→A→D. When newly appointed, your direct report can expect to have many ticks in the 'Recommend' column. As they gain experience these should be shifting across to 'Act' and subsequently to 'Delegate'.

This R/A/D system becomes still more interesting and fruitful if you have several direct reports doing similar work. They compile the list together and go through it with you as a group. A given decision may then be allocated to the 'R' column for James, who is new to the job; to 'A' for Sarah and Lesley, who are more experienced; and to 'D' for Barbara who has handled it many times.

A further variation of this system, which clears your own desk even more effectively, is for James to take any items in his 'Recommend' column not to you but to his colleague Barbara, who coaches him in moving from R to A. As manager of the team, you can scan the columns to see where the ticks fall for each person. If James has still kept most of the ticks under 'R' some months after starting the job, perhaps he needs some help to build his confidence; if Lesley has masses of items under 'A' it is time she learned to delegate more of them, and so on.

Delegating to a secretary or PA

Fewer and fewer managers are now entitled to a secretary or PA of their own. Many managers' own keyboard and IT skills are adequate for them to type their own correspondence, with e-mails increasingly replacing letters.

But if you have access, shared or exclusive, to a secretary/PA – who may be called team secretary, executive assistant or whatever – you have further opportunities for delegation. Surveys carried out by The Industrial Society regularly show that secretaries/PAs want to take on more accountability and are frustrated by a lack of delegation. How do you rate in the delegation stakes?

Exercise

Below are some tasks which you may be able to delegate to a secretary/PA – tick those that you do:

☐ *Managing your diary*

☐ *Ordering stationery and office equipment*

☐ *Arranging your travel and accommodation*

☐ *Processing your expenses*

☐ *Replying to routine correspondence*

☐ *Drafting replies to non-routine correspondence*

☐ *Taking the minutes in meetings*

☐ *Summarising articles and reports*

☐ *Carrying out research for your work, eg surfing the net*

☐ *Consulting other members of your team about options, and coming back to you with proposals*

☐ *Revising the filing system*

☐ *Planning the layout of the department for greater efficiency*

☐ *Progress-chasing, eg reminding people of deadlines*

☐ *Drafting questionnaires*

☐ *Form design*

☐ *Acting as a 'gatekeeper' to prevent you being interrupted*

☐ *Screening incoming mail and only passing to you those items which you need to see*

☐ *Operating a 'bring forward' system*

☐ *Preparing and updating visual displays, eg wall charts*

☐ *Gathering together relevant papers for meetings.*

The items on the above checklist are not those which serve your stakeholders. You are not operating at your added value level if you are personally performing them. So, be tough with yourself and delegate them!

Breaking through resistance

For some reason, among the worst offenders for holding on to these activities are professionally qualified people such as lawyers, accountants, surveyors, architects and academics. This is strange because they are supposed to be spending their time earning fees for their organisation.

An effective method of making the breakthrough is to ask a facilitator to lead a one-day workshop for a dozen secretaries/PAs. During the morning they generate lists of all the tasks which they could take over from their managers. During the afternoon those managers join the workshop and are presented with the lists. Their typical reaction is to come up with reasons why "it sounds fine in principle, but it would never work in practice".

The facilitator helps to build the managers' confidence that it can work – it's just that they have never tried it before. And the workshop ends with commitments to action rather than cop-outs such as "We'll give it further thought".

Consultation

Another opportunity for delegation arises in the context of consultation. Macho managers enjoy the sheer power of making decisions and regard it as tedious and time-consuming to consult those who will be affected by a decision.

Effective managers, on the other hand, make it clear to their teams that their general approach will be to involve the team as much as possible. Asking for suggestions simply enriches the quality of a decision, and it is worth bearing in mind this formula:

The quality of implementation of a decision = The quality of the decision-making x the commitment to make it happen.

You can express this more simply as:

Result = process x commitment.

As the formula shows, it is quite possible for the end result to be a minus quantity.

Of course, it is neither necessary nor sensible to involve your colleagues in every decision – operational urgency precludes that. But the following 'Seven degrees of consultation' provide a useful test of your attitude to delegation. By breaking the issue down into these layers you are giving yourself increasing scope to delegate.

Seven degrees of consultation

0   I have decided X – get on with it

1   I have decided X – let me have your feedback about it

2   I propose X, but you can fine tune it

3   I propose X, but I am prepared to consider Y

4   I propose X, but am prepared to consider other alternatives

5   Here is the issue. I would like your views before I decide

6   Here is the issue. What should we do? (Aiming towards consensus)

7   Here is the issue: you decide

Summary checklist

✓ Be aware of your own learning style and that of individual team members.

✓ Analyse regular decisions with your direct reports and use the Recommend/Act/Delegate approach.

✓ Go through the checklist with your PA/secretary.

8

Coaching

This chapter covers:
> Using questions and giving feedback.
> Putting yourself in the other person's shoes.
> The 'GROW' sequence.
> Example of a coaching dialogue.

What is coaching?

People often associate coaching with rectifying mistakes, but it is essentially about improving performance, even when performance is already good – notice how world champions in golf, swimming or tennis still have coaches. And notice also that a good coach does not have to be better at that activity than the person they are coaching: most coaches for heavyweight boxers appear to be about four feet tall and 70 years old, and could hardly climb into the ring let alone deliver a knockout punch!

A coach helps a person to perform more effectively. This could mean achieving higher output, or completing a task in a shorter time, or with less effort, or with better relationships with colleagues. So coaching is an invaluable skill in delegation.

Many managers claim to be coaching their people as a matter of course, but if they have never been trained to coach, or really thought hard about what true coaching involves, their version of coaching is likely to be well-meant but amateurish.

Coaching is not telling someone how to do something, but helping them to find the best way for themselves. A simple definition is:

Coaching is unlocking potential to maximise performance.

To coach someone in carrying out market research, or in compiling a report, or in repairing a faulty valve, you do not have to be particularly skilled at these tasks yourself. The most important element is your ability to help the person to analyse their own efforts.

Improving performance through coaching

You will enable a person to improve their performance significantly if you enhance their *awareness* of how they are carrying out a task, and their feeling of *control* over their performance.

To take the market research example, you can enhance their awareness of how they are tackling the research either by giving them direct feedback ("You seem to be assuming x") or by questioning them ("Are you making any assumptions about x?")

To take the example of repairing the valve, you can use direct feedback ("You seem to have placed the tools in an awkward position") or questioning ("Is that the most convenient place for the tools? Is there any alternative place for them?")

Whilst you may have to give them some direct feedback, the most profound impact on their performance is likely to result from questioning, because that makes them think it out for themselves and become aware, perhaps for the first time, of what they have been doing unconsciously.

When you are coaching, please bear in mind that:

- Your level of experience in the task may be different to the learner's.

- Your route to the destination may be different to theirs.

- Your learning style may be different to theirs.

It does not always follow that the greatest experts make the best coaches. If you are chief geologist for an oil company you can examine a seismological chart and quickly assess its potential for yielding oil. Someone who is a novice, however, may be struggling to make out anything meaningful from the data. You would probably find it difficult, if not impossible, to put yourself in their shoes, because the data looks so obvious to you. But that is what a good coach does: you put yourself in the other person's shoes and patiently enhance their awareness.

How coaching can help delegation

You will find that coaching has something valuable to offer, both at the stage when you are considering delegation but have not yet committed yourself, and once you have decided to take the plunge. Here is the first of these situations:

 *Case study*

Sarah is a team leader in a call centre. She has been coaching Jack, who has plenty of experience of telephone contact with customers through his work in his previous company, but who is climbing a steep learning curve about the requirements of his new employer's customers. From her coaching sessions Sarah already knows quite a lot about Jack's strengths and weaknesses. He has plenty of enthusiasm and can quickly establish friendly relationships on the phone. At present he is finding the breadth of the product range daunting and this is making him flustered when a customer asks for something slightly out of the ordinary.

Sarah decides to continue her coaching sessions, but also for the next six weeks to delegate to Jack a task which until now she has carried out personally – a weekly assessment of requests for products outside the central core. Jack is familiar with the 80/20 rule, which will be a useful tool for this task, and the assessment process is a PC-based job involving no direct customer contact, so Jack has no need to get flustered. By taking on the assessment Jack's product knowledge will be improved, which in turn will boost his confidence. Sarah's close contact with him via the coaching sessions will enable her to judge whether to make this piece of delegation permanent.

For an example of coaching where you have definitely decided to delegate, see the case study below which features the 'GROW' model.

The 'GROW' sequence

A very useful sequence for coaching is 'GROW': Goal, Reality, Options, Will. A manager has decided to delegate a task to one of his team, but first needs to be confident that she can handle it. They agree to spend half an hour talking it through, using the GROW sequence.

Example

In this example, David is the manager and Barbara is a member of his team. They work for a graphics design company. Once every three months or so the company hosts a reception for new and prospective clients, which includes displays of the company's work and provides an opportunity for informal discussion between clients and with the company's staff.

David: OK Barbara, let's talk about the reception coming up in June. Up to now I've always arranged these events, but I think you may be ready to take over. How do you feel about it?

Barbara: Yes, I'd like to have a go, but I'm going to need your guidance.

David: Right. So let's agree where we'll try to get to in this meeting as a start.

Barbara: Well, it would be good to go over what guidance I need between now and June, and also what help I will have on the day. **[Goal]**

David: Fine. So our aim is to agree how to help you prepare, and how to support you on June 14th. You've attended a couple of these receptions already, so you know roughly what happens. How confident are you about arranging it all?

Barbara: I've actually been to three receptions and the format was similar each time. I'm quite confident about the catering side – that always goes well because George has it beautifully organised. I suppose there are two aspects which I need help with. One is how to get the right balance between existing clients and potential clients. The other is the actual layout of the displays – at the last reception they seemed a bit cramped and I have a rough idea of how we might change that. **[Reality]**

David: OK, good. Let's focus on the client list. Here's the list from last time. The potential clients are starred.

Barbara: Yes – what I noticed was that several of the potentials didn't actually turn up, so it left clients who already knew each other talking together, which rather spoilt the point of the event.

David: Yes, I know what you mean. Any ideas about that? **[Options]**

Barbara: Well, I suppose we could invite three times as many potentials as we really need, rather like airlines deliberately overbooking because some people are 'no shows'. But it feels a bit risky…

David: Mmm. Any other ideas? **[Options]**

Barbara: Perhaps it would help if I looked through the lists for the last four or five receptions and check the proportion of potentials who don't turn up. That may give us a better steer for how many to invite in June.

David: OK, fine.

Barbara: When I've compiled the list to be invited in June, I'd welcome your comments on the personalities, so I'm forewarned about who to keep apart!

David: Right. Now what about your plans for the display area?

Barbara: Well, I haven't got any plan yet, more of a feeling that there's got to be a better answer.

David: Let's look at this diagram of the rooms we used last time. We had refreshments over here and the displays in the next room, mainly along that right-hand wall.

Barbara: Yes, I think there are two things that worry me – one is the amount of space, it just seemed cramped over at that side. The other is that some of the exhibits were much bigger than others, so it seemed off balance.

David: So how else could it be done? **[Options]**

Barbara: I could get together in a week or so with all the people who'll be preparing the exhibits and agree some tighter guidelines on the size of each exhibit, so we get more consistency.

David: Sounds good.

Barbara: And at that same meeting, I could take all of them together to have a look at the rooms we used last time, to see what better layout we could come up with.

David: OK. So let's recap where we've got to. Just run through the actions we've agreed.

Barbara: I'm going to look through the lists for previous receptions and decide the right number of invitations for June. Then you will help me with comments on the people who accept, to avoid personality clashes. I will meet the display team next week and agree new guidelines for the exhibits, and we'll come up with an improved display area.

David: That's fine. I'm sure you're ready to take this over now. On a scale of 1-10, how confident do you feel about it?

Barbara: Well, if you'd asked me half an hour ago I would have said about six. Now I think eight. **[Will]**

David: Right. I'd have been worried if you'd said 10! So it's all yours now, but ask if you need help, and we'll talk through those personalities nearer the time.

Barbara: Right. Thanks.

Summary checklist

✓ Increase your delegate's awareness and control.

✓ Put yourself in your delegate's shoes.

✓ Use the GROW sequence to help the delegate find the right route.

Following up after delegation

This chapter offers advice on:
> How to check without stifling people.
> Using regular 'one-to-ones'.

Checking, not stifling

Having taken the plunge and delegated a task to someone, you obviously want to check whether it has been successful. As we have seen, this should not be done by breathing down their neck while they carry out the task. It does not help if you become what Ted Johns once called a 'White-Shirted Hoverer' – a bird which delegates tasks to someone then perches on their shoulder while they carry them out.

'Exception reporting'

One option is to use 'exception reporting'. This is the principle of 'no news is good news', ie you will assume that things have gone well unless you hear from your delegate to the contrary. For relatively minor issues this may well be the best approach, because it doesn't waste any of your time or theirs.

The one-minute approach

The second approach is that described in *The One Minute Manager* (see Further Reading). An effective manager tries to "catch his employees doing something right" rather than the traditional method of trying to catch them out making mistakes. The one-minute approach entails you walking round your team's working area in an informal but observant way, and spending a brief period – perhaps literally a minute – with each individual, giving them a simple word of encouragement. If one of these encounters provides the opportunity to see your delegate successfully achieving the delegated activity, this is ideal.

'One-to-ones'

The third system is the regular progress review, often known simply as a 'one-to-one' or 'one-on-one' – a private discussion between you and your delegate.

In a surprising number of organisations this system is not yet in place. There will be an annual performance appraisal but nothing in between. The lack of 'one-to-ones' is usually 'justified' by the fact that the two of you have frequent contact anyway – in some situations, the individual and the manager sit at neighbouring desks or have adjacent offices.

But in many other situations, a person may not see their manager face-to-face for days or weeks on end. Field engineers, delivery drivers, account executives, district nurses, supply teachers – people in such posts operate 'out of sight' for much of their time, and the danger is that out of sight = out of mind.

So I recommend that you should have a one-to-one discussion with each of your direct reports at least once a quarter, regardless of how often you see them in between. These short, informal discussions give both of you the chance to stand back from the day-to-day detail and see how the work is progressing; review recent targets and set fresh ones; and take stock of how you work together.

One-to-ones should not be long, formal and paper-generating, but will prove very worthwhile if they fulfil the following eight criteria:

Criteria for successful one-to-ones

- A private, face-to-face discussion.
- The discussion reviews the whole of the job, not just a single aspect.
- The meeting is structured, not a casual chat.
- The discussion includes past, present and future: the usual timescale is up to three months in each direction.
- Although most of the discussion is about the delegate's work, you will invite them to make constructive comments on your method of managing and to take stock of your effectiveness as a partnership.
- You produce specific action points with deadline dates.
- You each make notes on the discussion, on one sheet of paper.
- At the end of the discussion you agree a date for the next one-to-one and this is entered on the notes.

An obvious item to include in a one-to-one is any recently delegated task. You can update your delegate's job description by adding the task, and deleting it from yours. If the delegation has been successful, does that suggest any other tasks currently handled by you which you may now feel ready to delegate – not necessarily to that delegate, but to some other member of your team?

And can you learn anything from the way the delegation process worked? If so, other members of the team may benefit if you share this learning with them.

Managers who review delegation in this way liken it to running an ongoing 'delegation clinic', producing fresh possibilities for other team members.

Learning from delegation

If you really want to learn from your delegation experience there are three ways of doing so. First, you can use feedback from your delegates: how it felt to them on the receiving end. Was the pace right? Did they feel you were rushing them at any stage – or did they feel impatient because you seemed over-cautious? Did they sense that you were seeing the issues through their eyes? What were your most helpful and least helpful interventions?

Second, you may be able to use a coach or a mentor: the former to enhance your awareness of your delegation style and your mastery of it; the latter to help you see delegation in perspective. Mentors tend to nudge people towards the strategic rather than the operational end of the spectrum, so they are particularly relevant in the delegation context: your mentor should be able to assist you to work nearer your true 'added value' level.

Third, you may find it revealing to keep a delegation diary. Whenever we review something which has engaged us over a significant period, our impressions about the final stages are naturally strongest. But there may be important lessons to be learned from the earlier phases, so it helps to keep a diary which captures how you felt **at the time** at each phase of the process. In particular, it can be invaluable to realise in retrospect what kept you on the right track at times of difficulty.

Summary checklist

✓ Use exception reporting as a simple way of following up.

✓ Encourage team members by brief contacts.

✓ Set up regular progress reviews on a 'one-to-one' basis.

✓ Update job descriptions to record transfers of accountability.

Conclusion

Delegation is a key skill in any organisation. The mechanics of how to carry it out are not very complicated; the aspects in which you are likely to need more help are in overcoming your hesitations about delegating, such as the fear of losing control or your worry that the delegate will make a stupid mistake. This book should have reassured you on these points.

If you follow the approaches we have outlined you should find that you have created a double benefit – you will have helped one of your team to grow and at the same time you will have freed yourself up to deliver your own optimum value to the organisation.

Be brave. Delegate.

Further reading/Bibliography

Coaching for Performance, Sir John Whitmore, Nicholas Brealey Publishing, 1996

Effective Coaching, Myles Downey, Orion Business, 1999

Effective Feedback Skills, Tim Russell, Kogan Page, 1998

Empowered, Rob Brown and Margaret Brown, Nicholas Brealey Publishing, 1994

Essential Delegation Skills, Carla Brown, Gower, 1997

Managing the Professional Service Firm, David Maister, Free Press, 1997

Managing Time, Debra Allcock Tyler, The Industrial Society, 2001

The Manual of Learning Styles, Peter Honey and Alan Mumford, Peter Honey Publications

The One Minute Manager, Keith Blanchard, HarperCollinsBusiness, 2000